Made in United States
North Haven, CT
18 May 2022

19288911R10057